Longhorn Football Legends

By Dave Sessions
Original cover art by Mark Hoffer

Great Texas Line Press
Fort Worth, Texas

Longhorn Football Legends

Copyright: Great Texas Line Press

For bulk sales
and whole inquiries
contact:
Great Texas Line Press
Post Office Box 11105
Fort Worth, TX 76110
greattexas@hotmail.com
www.greattexasline.com

To see our complete list of Texas guide, humor and cook books,
visit: www.greattexasline.com

Editor: Tom Johanningmeier
Cover and inside illustrations: Mark Hoffer
Copy Editor: John Henry
Printed by the Swiger family of Hanson Printing, Fort Worth

Great Texas Line Press strives to be socially responsible, donating a portion
of proceeds from several books to Habitat for Humanity of Fort Worth,
North Fort Worth Historical Society, Texas Dance Hall Preservation Inc.
and Terlingua's Big Bend Educational Foundation. Hundreds of books are
donated annually to public-radio stations throughout Texas for fund-rais-
ing. Every effort is made to engage Texas writers, editors, illustrators, de-
signers and photographers who fell victim to the newspaper industry
crisis, and to produce the books at local, family-run print shops.

Contents

Introduction

Few college football teams have as long and remarkable a history as the Texas Longhorns, from their humble beginnings before the turn of the 20th century, to their dominance under legendary coach Darrell Royal to their ascendance as a perennial powerhouse under Mack Brown.

Like the New York Yankees in baseball or the Dallas Cowboys in pro football, Texas is a team that inspires burning passion among both its fans and rivals. You can see that in the "Hook 'em Horns" sign, which is proudly waved by the Longhorns faithful and furiously pointed downward by legions of opposing fans without a hand signal of their own.

Nowadays, Darrell K Royal-Texas Memorial Stadium is an unending sea of burnt orange, 100,000 fans strong, and the Horns are so popular they have their own television network. Every year brings hope that Texas will win another national championship and every player hopes to be the next Earl Campbell, Ricky Williams, Vince Young, Tommy Nobis or Bobby Layne.

They say, "The Eyes of Texas are upon you, all the live long day." That may be true, but the eyes of the nation are upon Texas, too. What happens in Austin reverberates throughout the college football landscape — from the invention of the Wishbone offense to the slew of Longhorns on NFL rosters. (It's common to see 50 or more in any given season.)

There are as many stories about the Horns as there are spots on mascot Bevo's hide – more than could ever be captured in a book of any size. So here are some of the most interesting and most memorable Longhorns legends from Texas football.

— *Dave Sessions*

Starting small

Like most of the oldest college football programs in the country, Texas made its start on a sloppy field in front of a crowd small enough to fit into a gymnasium. It was 1893 and the University of Texas itself was only 10 years old.

The Dallas Football Club challenged UT to a game, the first of many Longhorn contests at what is now known as Fair Park in Dallas. And the UT squad of 15 or 16 strong (nobody knows for sure) defeated the so-called "Champions of Texas," 18-16 on Thanksgiving Day before 2,000 fans, the largest football crowd in Dallas history at the time.

What's in a name? The Bevo mystery

Fourteen Longhorn steers have served as Texas' official mascot, with the first taking his place on the field — less than enthusiastically — in November 1916 during halftime of the Texas A&M game. Bevo I was presented to the UT student body by a group of alumni. When it came time for his official photograph, Bevo charged the camera.

Cushing Memorial Library and Archives, Texas A&M University

The Aggies branded the Longhorn mascot with the score of their 1915 victory over Texas.

After the Horns downed the Aggies 22-7, Ben Dyer, the editor of the alumni magazine *Texas Alcalde*, wrote, "His name is Bevo. Long may he reign!"

But how did Bevo get his name?

A popular story, especially when Aggies tell it, is that after a group of A&M students branded Bevo with "13-0" to commemorate their 1915 victory over UT, embarrassed Longhorns changed the "13" to a "B," the dash to an "E" and inserted a "V."

Another legend says Bevo's moniker was inspired by a recently introduced non-alcoholic beer with the same name. But Bevo the beer wasn't yet selling well in Austin when Bevo the steer took on his name.

The most likely story, according to the folks at the Texas Exes, is that Bevo's name is a combination of "beeve," a slang term for a head of cattle that's destined to become food, and the then-common fad of adding "o" to the end of a name to create a nickname.

TRADITIONS
How 'Hook 'em Horns' happened

It's one of the most recognizable hand signals in sports: the index finger and pinky finger pointed to the sky to make the "Hook 'em Horns" sign. It's so well known that opposing teams and fans appropriate it in their own upside-down version. Longhorns fans teach their kids how to do it before they can even count.

Even President George W. Bush flashed the "Hook 'em Horns" during the parade at his second inauguration — much to the concern of Norwegians, for whom the sign means something different: Satan. (A Norwegian newspaper headline crowed, "Shock greeting from Bush daughter," when first daughter Jenna Bush, a UT grad, joined her family in the gesture to honor the Longhorn Band.)

The "Hook 'em Horns" dates to 1955, when UT cheerleader Harley Clark introduced the signal that his friend, Henry Pitts, had come up with and shown Clark a few days earlier. Clark brought "Hook 'em" to a pep rally and it took on a life of its own.

Clark, who went on to become a state district judge, said he was motivated to introduce a hand sign because Texas A&M already had been using the "Gig 'em" thumbs-up gesture for years.

Layne tames
the Tigers

If ESPN's *SportsCenter* had existed on Jan. 1, 1946, you can bet Bobby Layne would have been all over the highlights. The Longhorns downed Missouri in the Cotton Bowl, 40-27, and the Texas quarterback had a hand (or foot) in every point.

Layne, who would eventually become one of the NFL's greatest signal-callers of his era, threw for two touchdowns, ran for three touchdowns, caught a 50-yard touchdown bomb and kicked all four extra points. It seems the only thing Layne wasn't able to do is tackle a Tiger for a safety.

Layne's school records for career passing yards and passing TDs stood for nearly 40 years, and Layne's 28-6 record as a starter wasn't topped until Vince Young went 30-2 from 2003-05.

Super kicker

"Field-goal range" means different things to different kickers — usually in college, it's somewhere past the opponents' 25- or 30-yard line. For Russell Erxleben, field-goal range seemed to be from wherever they'd let him kick it.

The 6-foot-4, 215-pound Erxleben was a straight-on kicker in the era when soccer-style kicking was beginning to dominate, but his leg strength was such that he could simply back up, take a couple of strides and kick the ball to the stratosphere.

In 1977, late in an out-of-control blowout over Rice, Erxleben stepped into the record books with a 67-yard field goal. With an 8-12 mph wind at his back, Erxleben kicked what is still the longest field goal in NCAA history.

"I'll never forget the sound it made when he hit it, " coach Fred Akers said. "It sounded like a gun-

ROYALISM

"There's an old saying: You dance with who brung ya."

on the value of consistency

shot. ... We couldn't believe a ball was going that far. It had another eight yards on it."

Erxleben kicked two more 60-plus-yard field goals that season. He played six seasons in the NFL, mostly as a punter, and then found more controversial career choices. He was sentenced to seven years in prison for defrauding investors of $36 million in 1999, and he was indicted in early 2013 in connection with a Ponzi scheme involving a Gauguin painting.

Run, Ricky, run

Soft-spoken, dreadlocked and built like a boulder, Ricky Williams ran his way into the history books during his UT tenure as well as a prolific NFL career.

Ricky Williams

Though he was recruited out of San Diego by coach John Mackovic, Williams became a crucial piece of coach Mack Brown's rebuilding project in 1998, when Williams led the NCAA in rushing for the second consecutive season.

Though he would certainly have been a high draft pick, Williams stayed for his senior season, Brown's first at Texas. By the time Williams was done, he held 21 NCAA records and 46 school records. He left UT with the NCAA record for career rushing yards (6,279), all-purpose yards (7,206), rushing TDs (72) and total TDs (75).

Longhorns fans will always remember Williams' most impressive highlight: topping Tony Dorsett's NCAA rushing record by breaking three tackles on a 60-yard run against Texas A&M in the final game of the 1998 regular season.

Williams won the Heisman Trophy in 1998 and was the first player to win the Doak Walker Award, presented to the nation's top running back, in back-to-back seasons. For his career, Williams averaged an astounding 6.2 yards per carry.

In 2012, the Longhorns unveiled a statue of Williams outside Darrell K Royal-Texas Memorial Stadium and Brown brought Williams to his team's running backs meeting.

"They were just in awe," Brown said. "Just bringing a rock star in and walking him into the running back room. They were sitting up front and I walked in and said, 'This is Ricky Williams.' They couldn't move. They just sat there. They didn't say 'hello.' They didn't shake his hand."

Tyler Rose vs. Bevo

Earl Campbell was the Longhorns' first Heisman Trophy winner in 1977 and a punishing power runner who later ran roughshod over NFL defenders for eight seasons.

He also holds the distinction of being the only running back brave enough, fast enough and strong enough to plow into the Longhorns' nearly one-ton bovine mascot, Bevo.

After a touchdown run into the corner of the end zone, Campbell bowled into Bevo with such a head of steam that the poor steer almost went down in a heap.

"Bevo took most of the blow," Campbell told *Sports Illustrated*. "He didn't fall, but I could feel him stumble backward. After he got his balance, he looked at me and said, 'Moo.'"

Peter the Great

The Texas-Oklahoma rivalry has been one-sided at times — in the 2000s, usually leaning to the north side — and it has featured a slew of standout quarterbacks. OU even had two Heisman Trophy winners under center on their dominant teams of the 2000s.

But no one quarterback ever owned the Red River Rivalry — played each October at Dallas' Cotton Bowl during the State Fair of Texas — the way Texas' Peter Gardere did from

Peter Gardere

1989-92. Gardere started four games against the Sooners and beat them all four times, making him the only quarterback in more than a century of Texas-OU meetings to accomplish that feat.

Gardere didn't even have the luxury of leading spectacular Texas squads or playing against mediocre Oklahoma teams. Far from it — the Horns were unranked each time, while the Sooners were ranked 16th or better each time.

In '89 and '90, Gardere's redshirt freshman and sophomore seasons, the young QB from Houston led the Longhorns to fourth-quarter comebacks over OU. In '91, the Longhorns won just 10-7. And by Gardere's senior year, when Texas won by a relatively comfortable 10-point margin, OU fans were consoling themselves with a Fletcher's Corny Dog on the fair grounds and the solace that they would never, ever have to see Peter Gardere take another snap against them.

"I heard our fans yelling, 'Four more years!' as I left the field and I heard the Oklahoma fans yelling, "Graduate, graduate!'" Gardere said after the game. "I had to crack a smile at that."

Colt McCoy's first miracle

Longhorns fans will never forget what Colt McCoy did for them as he racked up the most wins ever by a UT quarterback. But Ken Herrington will always remember him for a different reason: McCoy may have saved his life.

Colt McCoy

Herrington was McCoy's neighbor on the other side of a 300-yard lake north of Graham, a small town 110 miles or so northwest of Dallas. He had worked at NASA before a brain hemorrhage forced him into early retirement.

On Memorial Day 2006, Herrington, then 60, suffered a seizure on his dock. Herrington's dog barked and his wife, Patina, screamed. McCoy, then 19, sprung into action.

McCoy and his father, Brad, swam across the lake. A neighbor called 911. But Colt's deeds weren't done. The dock was more than a quarter-mile down a rocky path from the county road. McCoy, barefoot and with only a flashlight, climbed up the path and helped lead paramedics down the path.

While Ken was recovering, Patina emailed the story to the media (neither Colt nor Brad had shared it).

"It was just a true hero story of how everybody came together and saved a life," she told The Associated Press.

And thus began the legend of Colt McCoy.

He won the starting job over Jevan Snead that fall and never surrendered it, going on to become college football's top quarterback in his junior and senior years. From 2006-09, McCoy set school records in career touchdown passes, single-season touchdown passes, total touchdowns by a Texas player, career wins and career passing yards.

Cover boys

Tommy Nobis was one of the greatest line-backers in college football history, a two-time All-American and a two-way player who started on both sides of the ball. Maybe that's why he was face of the Longhorns during his tenure: He was featured on the covers of *Life* and *Sports Illustrated* in 1965.

No Longhorns magazine cover can match the Nov. 17, 1941, *Life* cover, though. In classic *Life* style, the red-and-white lettering sat atop over the black-and-white photography, but instead of a single photo, the magazine ran 14 mugshots of UT players with the simple headline, "Texas football."

According to the *Austin American-Statesman*, that '41 bunch was the first Texas team to reach the No. 1 ranking, the first to have a consensus All-American, the first to win the hat-inspired trophy for the winner of the Texas-OU game and the first to inspire the "Hex Rally" practice of burning red candles before the A&M game.

Cowboys coach was Horns hero

Before Tom Landry roamed the Dallas Cowboys' sideline in his trademark fedora, he roamed the backfield in a Longhorns helmet. No UT alumnus ever achieved more as a coach than Landry, a master innovator and contributor to the NFL's growth in the 1960s and 1970s — and the onetime Longhorns fullback learned a lot from his collegiate coaches, Dana X. Bible and Blair Cherry.

Bible "was a great orator and motivator," said Landry, who was co-captain of the 1948 Longhorns squad. "Some of his locker-room talks were pure Knute Rockne ... a great organizer and the greatest recruiter I ever saw."

Landry's finest moment as a Longhorn may have been his final game, the 1949 Orange Bowl. He rushed for 117 yards on 17 carries in a

TRADITIONS
Orange and white

In 1900, the UT regents officially selected orange and white as the school colors after an election for students, faculty, staff and alumni. Before that, according to the Texas Exes, various Longhorn sports teams took the field in all sorts of colors: yellow, orange, white, red, maroon and blue among them.

The characteristic burnt orange color didn't come around until 1928, when football coach Clyde Littlefield ordered a new shade that wouldn't fade (the jerseys were more yellow than orange by the end of every season). But the Great Depression made dye expensive and Texas went back to bright orange until coach Darrell Royal brought back burnt orange for good in the 1962 season.

high-scoring upset over highly ranked Georgia.

Landry's worst moment at Texas, on the other hand, was in 1947, when he slipped and fell in the mud before he could take a handoff from quarterback Bobby Layne on fourth-and-1 in the Horns' only loss that season.

"I can still see the funny look on [Layne's] face, standing there with nobody to give the ball to," Landry said decades later.

After his time at Texas, Landry starred for the New York Giants as a player, then became a coach after seven pro seasons. He went on to invent the 4-3 defense and lead the Cowboys for 29 seasons. He won two Super Bowls, five NFC titles and 270 total games, the third-most in NFL history.

ROYALISM

 "Give me an O.J. Simpson, and I'll show you a coaching genius."

on what it takes to be a great coach

Keeping up with the Joneses

It's not uncommon for teams to have two players with the same last name, necessitating the use of a first initial on the back of the jersey to keep things straight.

In 1977, though, Texas had three great players named Jones. Coach Fred Akers had to come up with nicknames to differentiate the three: Johnny Jones was "Lam" because he was from Lampasas; Johnny Jones was "Ham" because he was from Hamlin; and Anthony Jones of Ohio was "Jam," because, well, just because.

"Those are three of the most recognizable names in college football," Jam Jones said.

When Ham was a senior, Lam was a junior and Jam was a freshman, the Joneses made a remarkable combo in the 1977 Sun Bowl victory over

Maryland. The three combined for 211 yards in a 42-0 win. Ham rushed for 109 yards on 14 carries and was named the game's MVP; Lam scored on a reverse and caught a 29-yard TD pass, and Jam rushed 19 times for 100 yards.

The Jones boys scored five touchdowns that day, prompting an Alabama newspaper to write the classic headline, "Jam, Ham and Lam put the wham on Maryland." Asked about it years later, Jam said, "Man, we cut up that game."

TRADITIONS
'Eyes of Texas'

Now a fixture after all games, wins and losses, *The Eyes of Texas*, UT's alma mater, was written by John Lang Sinclair in 1903. Set to the tune of "I've Been Working on the Railroad," the lyrics were a nod to university president, Lamdin Prather, who often told students "the eyes of Texas are upon you" as he exhorted them to make the state proud with their actions. *The Eyes* is played before and after every Longhorns sporting event and at all other official university functions.

The trailblazer

Amid all the superlatives that can be said about the legendary 1969 Longhorns team, there's one uncomfortable truth: It was the last all-white team to win a national college football championship.

Fortunately for Texas, Julius Whittier was waiting in the wings. As a freshman when Texas won in 1969, Whittier was ineligible to play (freshmen in those days weren't allowed to play varsity competition) — but he was the lone black

Julius Whittier

player on the Longhorns squad, and would be their first black letterman and the UT version of Jackie Robinson the next season.

Of course, while Robinson had broken the baseball color barrier more than 20 years before, college football teams in the south were slow to integrate. When No. 1 Texas defeated No. 2 Arkansas in 1969, neither team had a black player.

Coach Darrell Royal had tried unsuccessfully to bring a few black players into the fold. Austinite Don Baylor (later an MLB great) wanted to play baseball and basketball in addition to football, so Royal lost out to the Baltimore Orioles.

Two other black student-athletes made the team but didn't stay more than a year.

That left Whittier to make history. The San Antonio native, an offensive lineman, became a three-year letterman and started his junior and senior years. Perhaps more important, he paved the way for future superstars like Roosevelt Leaks, who came to UT in 1971, and Earl Campbell, who arrived in 1974.

But while the next round of black Longhorn stars were well received at UT, Whittier was barely welcome on his own team. His teammates shunned him socially, and Royal even had difficulty finding Whittier a roommate before his sophomore season. Eventually, senior Billy Dale volunteered to live with Whittier — and that choice cost Dale, a popular player who admitted decades later that he "lost all his friends" because he was willing to share his room with a black man.

Whitter persevered, though, earning a master's degree at the UT school of public affairs. He became a lawyer, but he will always be best known for his contribution to the civil rights movement as a Longhorn.

"You know that football is a religion in Texas," he told the *New York Times*. "God and the university had the right people in the right places to handle my situation. It turned out to be a small event in the long and luminous life of a great and valuable institution."

Make a Wish(bone)

Heading into the 1968 season, the Long-horns had come off three mediocre seasons in which they lost a total of 12 games and appeared in only one bowl game. Their offense fell below 20 points per game in each of the previous two years.

Looking for something different, coach Darrell Royal instructed new offensive coordinator Emory Bellard, a veteran Texas high school coach, to develop a formation that would take advantage of the Horns' deep backfield. What Bellard came up with didn't merely change the Longhorns' fortunes: It changed football. The Wishbone offense featured the quarterback and three runners lined up in the shape of a "Y." Quarterbacks running the 'Bone had all kinds of options: hand to the fullback, fake to the fullback,

ROYALISM

"I've always felt that three things can happen to you when you throw the football, and two of them are bad.

on the value of a good running game

pitch to a tailback or take the back upfield himself, or some combination of the above. Triple option offenses existed before the Wishbone, but the new formation was designed to allow a more balanced attack.

The results weren't immediate — Texas tied its first game using the newfangled offense and lost its second — but then things clicked. The Longhorns won 30 consecutive games, an undisputed national championship in 1969 and a shared national title in 1970.

The two coaches' stroke of genius wasn't complete until after a game or two, as Royal recalled in the 2005 book *Coach Royal: Conversations With*

a Texas Football Legend. Royal wanted to call it the "Y" formation, but *Houston Chronicle* sportswriter Mickey Herskowitz told Royal, "That's not very original. Why don't you call it a 'wishbone'?"

Royal complied, and seven teams won or shared national titles from 1969-79 running Bellard's and Royal's creation.

$100 million team

The Texas Longhorns are college football's most valuable team, according to *Forbes.* In 2011, they also became the first team to generate more than $100 million, more than doubling the 2003 figure. Their revenues of $103.8 million topped second-place Alabama by almost $22 million.

Year	Revenue	Profit
2011	$103.8	$77.9
2010	$95.7	$71.2
2009	$93.9	$68.8
2008	$87.6	$65
2007	$73	$53
2005	$63.8	$46.2
2004	$53.2	$38.7
2003	$47.6	$34.7

Rolling the dice
on 'Roll Left'

John Mackovic won't go down in history as the Longhorns' most beloved head coach — perhaps his truest legacy was being so bad in 1997 that it compelled Texas to hire his successor, Mack Brown. Still, Mackovic made one of the gutsiest calls in Longhorns lore in his second-to-last year on the sidelines.

In 1996, the first year of the Big 12, Texas fell to 3-4 before rattling off four wins in a row, including a 51-15 demolition of Texas A&M to earn a berth in the new conference's first championship game, played at the Trans World Dome in St. Louis.

The Horns were heavy underdogs against No. 3 Nebraska, which seemed destined to vie for a third consecutive national championship. Instead

ROYALISM

"You've got to be in position for luck to happen. Luck doesn't go around looking for stumblebum."

of a blowout, though, the Cornhuskers found themselves in a fiercely contested battle with quarterback James Brown's feisty Longhorns.

The Horns held onto a 30-27 lead with 2:40 left in the game but faced fourth-and-inches on their own 28-yard line.

Going for it would have been risky. Turning the ball over would put Nebraska in position for a game-tying field goal or worse, a game-winning drive.

Mackovic rolled the dice with a play called "Roll Left." It was a bootleg, designed for the speedy Brown to outrun the defense, who, like everyone else in America, expected a safe quarterback sneak.

ABC television broadcaster Brent Musburger summed up expectations as Brown walked under center: "No question what's about to happen."

What nobody expected, except maybe Brown and sophomore tight end Derek Lewis, was that Brown would not only roll outside, but would stop and throw to a wide-open Lewis downfield. No Huskers defender was within 10 yards of Lewis, who raced all the way to the Nebraska 11.

Priest Holmes scored on the next play, giving Texas its first Big 12 championship. "Roll Left" was voted College Football's Play of the Year.

"That's the kind of call that makes you a hero," said UT athletic director DeLoss Dodds.

Of course, heroism can be short-lived at Texas. Dodds fired Mackovic a little more than a year later after a dismal 4-7 season.

TRADITIONS
An iconic logo

Here's a test: Drive around any Texas city for 15 minutes. If you don't see a Longhorns logo on the back of another car, you must be in College Station, because the silhouetted steer head is so ubiquitous you almost take it for granted. It's everywhere on Longhorn gear and is festooned throughout the university. And its most prominent position is the same place it first appeared: on the side of the Longhorns' white helmet.

On Sept. 23, 1961, the Horns took the field in Berkeley, Calif., wearing the new helmets with the logo that coach Darrell Royal had asked sporting-goods maven William "Rooster" Andrews to design.

When Andrews handed Royal a crayon drawing of the now-famous Longhorn head, the coach reportedly exclaimed, "This is it! And can we put it on a helmet?"

In the five decades that followed, Texas has put Andrews' logo on everything. In 2012, the University of Texas was the top seller of licensed college merchandise in the country, according to the Collegiate Licensing Company. Nearly $10 million in Longhorns merchandise is sold every year.

In-state hate:
Horns vs. Aggies

No rivalry has defined the Longhorns over the years more than their in-state feud with the Texas A&M Aggies. The contrast between the schools couldn't be greater: A&M is located in a country outpost and is known for its conservative, military background. UT sits in the ever-enlarging, cosmopolitan capital of Texas. That they happen to be the two largest universities in the state only adds to the rivalry. The two teams started playing football in 1894 and battled every year from 1915-2011, when the Aggies left the Big 12 Conference for the Southeastern Conference.

The *Aggie War Hymn*, A&M's unofficial fight song, is unusually preoccupied with its archrivals in Austin, referencing the Longhorns' uniform colors, their alma mater and their horns, which the

ROYALISM

"Football doesn't build character. It eliminates the weak ones."

Aggies hope to "saw off." Often in Texas, you'll see a pickup truck with no A&M stickers but a giant "sawed off" Longhorn logo. It seems some A&M fans hate the Horns more than they love the Aggies.

Why all this vitriol? Perhaps it's Texas' 76-37-5 record in the series. For now, until and unless the two resume their series in a nonconference meeting, the Longhorns have the last laugh: They defeated the Aggies, 27-25, in the 2011 game on a last-second field goal before a stunned sellout crowd at A&M's Kyle Field.

TRADITIONS
Super-sized stadium

Texas plays in the 100,119-seat Darrell K Royal-Texas Memorial Stadium on the east side of campus. There are more seats at "DKR" than even Cowboys Stadium, though Jerry Jones' palatial digs in Arlington hold more fans counting standing-room patrons.

When it was built as Memorial Stadium in 1924, the Horns' home held only 27,000 fans, but that was enough to let Texas bill it as the largest sports facility of its kind in the southwest. Capacity was at 47,000 fans by 1954, when lights were added, and a massive upper deck on the west side pushed the number of seats to almost 78,000 in 1971.

But the most impressive renovations to DKR have come in the past 20 years. The upper deck now wraps around like a horseshoe — and in the end zone without an upper deck, a giant, 136-foot-wide HD screen known as "Godzillatron" stands to entertain and interact with fans.

Plans eventually call for enclosing the entire upper deck and making room for 125,000 fans — more than any other non-racing stadium in the western world.

Stealing Reveille

In 1993, UT student Neil Andrew Sheffield read a *Dallas Morning News* article glorifying Reveille, Texas A&M's canine mascot, and decided he needed to take action.

The story said the Aggies' beloved collie was the only mascot in the Southwest Conference never to have been stolen, something Sheffield simply couldn't abide.

Soon, Sheffield and fellow Longhorn Paul Murray hatched a plan for a heist worthy of a *Mission Impossible* film. They would join forces with a contingent of about 30 other UT students, mostly Longhorn Band members, to distract and overpower Reveille's student handler while they were on the road at TCU.

Despite walkie-talkies and code words, their plan failed. But Sheffield, undeterred, found out the handler would be in Dallas over the winter break. Just after 6 a.m., Sheffield's break came when he saw Reveille alone in the backyard.

He lured the dog into his car and drove to Austin pondering his unprecedented raid.

"All I could think about was that I had just done something no one else has done, and there are 20,000 guys that would kick my ass," Sheffield told *The Daily Texan*, UT's student newspaper, more than a decade later, after he finally felt he was safe to reveal his identity. "It was like robbing Fort Knox. It was so cool."

A&M didn't acknowledge the dognapping, so Sheffield called the *Austin American-Statesman* a few days later to announce the news. The Aggies ultimately admitted Reveille was gone, and Sheffield, having proved his point, returned her by tying her to a post outside Lake Travis. He called the police and sped off just in time to evade the law.

Sheffield was lucky he didn't get caught: stealing a dog worth more than $1,500 would have been a felony, punishable by years in prison. And Reveille brought in enough marketing revenue to be valued at more than a million dollars.

For Sheffield, it's a good thing the statute of limitations is five years.

Bevo leaves his mark

Longhorns fans don't have much to reminisce about the 1999 Big 12 Championship game, as Texas never really had a chance in a 22-6 loss to the Nebraska Cornhuskers.

But the UT faithful did get one moment to cheer late in the game as Bevo XIII was led off the field. Sauntering gingerly behind his handlers, the old steer crossed the end zone emblazoned with "NE-BRASKA" on his way to his trailer.

There's no delicate way to say it: Bevo dropped his opinion of his opponents all over the big, red letters. That got the Texas fans roaring, if only for a moment — and it got the national TV broadcasters howling as they showed the replay.

The Alamodome groundskeepers sprang to work immediately, but Bevo had made his mark.

Who is this guy?

The plot sounds like something out of an Adam Sandler movie: a 30-year-old guy pretends to be someone else so he can keep playing college football long after his eligibility runs out. He manages to fool everybody at one of the most prestigious college programs in the nation ... and he almost gets by with it, only to be exposed on the eve of a major bowl game.

It would make a funny movie, but it really happened at Texas. Ron Weaver, 30, started his collegiate career at Monterey Peninsula College in 1984 and played at Sacramento State in 1988. By 1989, he had no eligibility — and he wasn't good enough to play pro football.

Weaver helped run the family liquor store for a while. He started volunteering as an unpaid assistant with Monterey Peninsula, his first team. And then, Weaver had an epiphany. Much like Dustin

Hoffman in *Tootsie*, the only thing keeping him from getting his dream job was that he was not someone else.

Weaver hatched up a scheme wherein he would use a friend's name and Social Security number to enroll at a junior college near Los Angeles, where he stood out sufficiently to get the attention of UT recruiters.

Now known as 23-year-old Ron McKelvey, the imposter made it through admissions at UT and eventually earned a full scholarship, though he didn't see much action. He played special teams and distinguished himself mostly for being beat for a touchdown late in a blowout, costing the Horns a shutout in a 48-7 win over Texas Tech.

By his final season at Texas, Weaver had played for four college teams over seven seasons. He even thought about redshirting another year just to stick awhile longer, but it was not meant to be.

Weaver had left too many crumbs behind on his trail of deception. Acting on an anonymous tip, Weaver's hometown paper in Salinas, Calif., outed him in a story on Dec. 30, 1995 — the day before Texas was to play Virginia Tech in the Sugar Bowl.

Weaver skipped town before the game. If it had been a Hollywood comedy, Texas would have won anyway. Instead the Longhorns, many of whom later admitted they were a bit rattled by the revelation that one of their own was a con man, lost 28-10.

The story, bizarre as it was, basically ended there. Though they unknowingly used an ineligible player, the Horns didn't have to worry about forfeiting games as Weaver's impact was negligible. The NCAA didn't (or perhaps couldn't) pursue any action against Weaver, and neither he nor the real McKelvey faced criminal charges over the Social Security fraud as apparently both were in on the scam.

All that was left was for Weaver to tell his story to *Sports Illustrated*, which he did a couple of weeks after the Sugar Bowl.

"If you asked me if I still wanted to play football tomorrow," he told *SI*, "I'd say yes."

The championships

1963
Win over Aggies brings first title

The Longhorns clinched their first national title with a tense 15-13 victory over Texas A&M at Kyle Field. Texas was the only undefeated team in college football entering that contest, so all it needed was a seventh consecutive victory over A&M to be declared the national champ.

Given that the

Sept. 20	at Tulane	W, 21-0
Sept. 28	Texas Tech	W, 49-7
Oct. 5	Okla. State	W, 34-7
Oct. 12	Oklahoma	W, 28-7
Oct. 19	at Arkansas	W, 17-13
Oct. 26	Rice	W, 10-6
Nov. 2	at SMU	W, 17-12
Nov. 9	Baylor	W, 7-0
Nov. 16	TCU	W, 17-0
Nov. 28	at Texas A&M	W, 15-13
Jan. 1	Navy	W, 28-6

Aggies had won only two games entering the rivalry meeting, a Texas title seemed a forgone conclusion. But A&M put up a fight on a field that was a barely playable mixture of mud and green paint for the national TV cameras. It was so bad that UT Board of Regents member Frank Erwin released a bombastic statement in the press box at halftime: "The condition of the playing field is a disgrace and a reflection on A&M. No university which makes any pretense of having a major athletic program would permit any such condition to exist."

It's likely Erwin's rage was exacerbated by the fact that A&M led UT 7-3 at halftime — and 13-3 after three quarters. The Horns soon capitalized on a fumble recovery for a TD, but failed on the 2-point conversion and trailed 13-9. Texas took advantage of another A&M lost fumble and won the game on Duke Carlisle's 1-yard quarterback sneak with 1:19 to play.

Though they were already officially national champions, the Longhorns faced No. 2 Navy, led by future Dallas Cowboys hero Roger Staubach, in the Cotton Bowl. They routed the Midshipmen, 28-6, to ensure there was no debate about 1963's top team.

1969
'Game of the Century' caps season

As the 100th season of college football wound to a close, the Longhorns and their toughest Southwest Conference foe, the Arkansas Razorbacks, were ranked first and second in the nation.

Everybody in the sport knew that year's Horns-Hogs game would be a momentous battle. Both teams entered the '69 season on a winning streak; Texas had won nine in a row the year

Sept. 20	at California	W, 17-0
Sept. 27	Texas Tech	W, 49-7
Oct. 4	Navy	W, 56-17
Oct. 11	vs Oklahoma	W, 27-17
Oct. 25	Rice	W, 31-0
Nov. 1	at SMU	W, 45-14
Nov. 8	Baylor	W, 56-14
Nov. 15	TCU	W, 69-7
Nov. 27	at Texas A&M	W, 49-12
Dec. 6	at Arkansas	W, 15-14
Jan. 1	Notre Dame	W, 21-17

before and one of those wins was Arkansas' only loss. Both teams ended the season in the AP poll's top 10.

Hoping the two teams would be undefeated against all their other opponents, ABC television wanted the marquee matchup to be played on the final Saturday of the season instead of the usual October meeting. To sweeten the deal, the network would have President Richard Nixon attend the game and personally bestow the national championship upon the winner.

Sure enough, the game that came to be known the "Big Shootout" and the "Game of the Century" would feature the two top-ranked teams in the nation, both undefeated. No. 1 Texas had won 18 games in a row; No. 2 Arkansas had won 15.

Amid all the hype and the wintry December weather, the Hogs took a 14-0 lead into the fourth quarter. But Texas QB James Street scrambled for a touchdown on the first play of the fourth, and then scored on a 2-point conversion as coach Darrell Royal had boldly decided before the game that he'd go for 2 to avoid a tie in a contest of such magnitude.

Arkansas had a chance to put the game away, driving to the Texas 7, but Danny Lester intercepted a Chuck Dicus pass to prolong the drama.

Then, on fourth-and-3 at UT's own 43, Darrell Royal, the notoriously conservative coach who es-

ROYALISM

"There are some people around here who think all we have to do is put on an orange uniform, crawl out there in the Wishbone and say, 'Bang, you're dead.'"

chewed the pass when possible, called the "right 53 veer" pass during a timeout before the play. Royal went for broke, betting the national title on the chance that a deep pass would succeed. And Street connected with Randy Peschel, who gained 44 yards after making a sensational, over-the-shoulder catch in double coverage.

Jim Bertelsen ran in the game-winning touchdown and Texas held off an Arkansas comeback bid to earn the right to meet the president.

In a televised locker-room speech, Nixon told the Texas players and coaches, "You won a tough one. For a team to be behind 14 to nothing and then not to lose its cool and to go on to win, that proves that you deserve to be No. 1, and that is what you are."

Nixon also said it was "one of the great games of all time, without a question." It is still considered a classic to this day, so much so that it has been the subject of a book (*Horns, Hogs, & Nixon Coming*, by Terry Frei) and a documentary (*The Big Shootout*, by filmmaker Mike Looney).

"Seldom, if ever, have I ever been interviewed about another close game," Royal said in the documentary during one of his last interviews before his death in 2012. "This is the only one folks still talk about."

1970
Winning streak reaches 30 games

Fresh off its undefeated 1969 championship season, Texas entered 1970 on a 20-game winning streak and rattled off 10 more in a row to clinch the top spot in the UPI poll as the regular season ended.

Texas was rarely tested in the regular season in 1970. The Longhorns defeated opponents by an av-

Sept. 19	California	W, 56-15
Sept. 26	at Texas Tech	W, 35-13
Oct. 3	UCLA	W, 20-17
Oct. 10	vs. Oklahoma	W, 41-9
Oct. 24	at Rice	W, 45-21
Oct. 31	at SMU	W, 42-15
Nov. 7	at Baylor	W, 21-14
Nov. 14	at TCU	W, 58-0
Nov. 26	Texas A&M	W, 52-14
Dec. 5	Arkansas	W, 42-7
Jan. 1	Notre Dame	L, 11-24

erage score of 41-15. The Horns' only close call was against UCLA in Week 3, when they had to come from behind on a TD pass to Cotton Speyrer with 12 seconds left to secure a 20-17 victory. Top-ranked Texas held off a spirited Bears team at Baylor in the seventh game and then cruised

ROYALISM

"A little bit of perfume doesn't hurt you if you don't drink it."

on handling praise after Texas' 30th consecutive victory in 1970

through blowout victories over TCU, A&M and No. 4 Arkansas — there was no "Game of the Century" this time as the Horns crushed the Hogs, 42-7.

But the Longhorns' good fortunes ran out on New Year's Day, 1971, when they met Notre Dame in the Cotton Bowl Classic for the second year in a row. This time, the Irish forced nine Texas fumbles and quarterback Joe Theismann led Notre Dame to a 24-11 victory that wasn't as close as the score.

Later that night, third-ranked Nebraska defeated fifth-ranked LSU in the Orange Bowl, giving the Cornhuskers the AP title after No. 1 Texas and No. 2 Ohio State had lost their bowl games earlier. But the UPI crowned its champion before bowl season through the 1973 season, so the Horns could count 1970 as their third title in the past eight seasons.

University of Texas

Vince Young's late fourth-down touchdown gave Texas the national championship.

2005
Young delivers win over mighty USC

Long before ESPN launched the Longhorn Network, the self-proclaimed "Worldwide Leader in Sports" seemed to have morphed into the Trojan Network. In the last few weeks of 2005, as a Texas-USC Rose Bowl championship match-up loomed, all the experts on ESPN (and many of them in print and elsewhere on the air) were trying to decide where that USC squad fit among the best teams of all time.

Sept. 3	La.-Lafayette	W, 60-3
Sept. 10	at Ohio State	W, 25-22
Sept. 17	Rice	W, 51-10
Oct. 1	at Missouri	W, 51-20
Oct. 8	vs Oklahoma	W, 45-12
Oct. 15	Colorado	W, 42-17
Oct. 22	Texas Tech	W, 52-17
Oct. 29	at Okla. State	W, 47-28
Nov. 5	Kansas	W, 66-14
Nov. 25	at Texas A&M	W, 40-29
Dec. 3	Colorado	W, 70-3
Jan. 4	USC	W, 41-38

One after another, a parade of ex-jocks and broadcasting school graduates stared solemnly into the camera and asked whether the No. 1 Trojans, winners of 34 consecutive games, were the *best team ever*?

On Jan. 5, 2006, the Longhorns proved they were better. Quarterback Vince Young turned in a dazzling, historic performance, rushing for 200 yards and passing for 267. No play that night — or perhaps in the history of UT football — was more memorable than Young's fourth-and-5 TD scramble to the right pylon of the end zone to cap a spectacular comeback drive and propel the Horns to a 41-38 victory.

So USC wasn't college football's best team ever, but Young had staked his claim as one of its best players.

Mack Brown

"A year and a half ago, people questioned whether he could be a quarterback, and now he has two Rose Bowl MVPs," Texas coach Mack Brown said after Young held aloft the BCS championship and the game MVP trophies. "He's one of the greatest players to ever play college football."

Sports Illustrated called Young's night "perhaps the most stunning bowl performance ever."

Young didn't win the 2006 Rose Bowl by himself, of course. The Texas defense supplied a pivotal stop just before Young led the final drive. USC coach Pete Carroll chose to go for it on fourth-and-2 at the Texas 45 with 2:13 to play, but the Horns stopped running back LenDale White just short and gave Young the chance to go to work.

Nobody's perfect

Texas has only had 13 losing seasons in more than a century of play, but there have been some UT squads that just plain stunk. So which was the worst Texas team? Here are four malodorous candidates:

1956
(1-9, seventh in Southwest Conference)

It's hard to imagine what Longhorn nation would do if a modern-day Texas team were as bad as the '56 bunch. Fans would probably storm the stadium with pitchforks and torches if they had a team that scored only 10.1 points per game while surrendering 27.2 points per game. The Horns' only win was a 7-6 squeaker over Tulane in Week 2. Texas did not win a SWC game and finished last in the conference. Not surprisingly, 1956 was coach Edwin Price's last at UT. Darrell Royal took over the next season and led the Horns to the Sugar Bowl.

1938
(1-8, seventh in SWC)

Coach Dana X. Bible took over in 1937 after Texas had endured two losing seasons in a row, and it was slow going at first for the future College Football Hall of Fame coach. His Horns went 2-6-1 in his first season, then regressed to 1-8 in 1938, averaging just 5.8 points per game (115th out of 122 college teams that year). The Longhorns lost their first nine games — averaging just three points per — but finally won, 7-6, in the final game of the year against Texas A&M. Bible turned Texas around the next year, culminating in the "Renaissance Game," when the Horns upset the No. 1-ranked Aggies at Kyle Field to clinch a 5-4 winning season.

ROYALISM

"There was a hornet's nest waiting for us in Houston, and we were walking into it like Little Red Riding Hood with Jam on her face."
after a 1958 loss to Rice

1988
(4-7, sixth in SWC)

The Horns started the season ranked No. 19, but Brigham Young trounced them 47-6 in the opener — and that wasn't even the season's worst blowout. Texas won close games over Rice (0-11 that year) and TCU (4-7), but was embarrassed by Houston, 66-15, in Austin.

1997
(4-7, fourth in Big 12 South division)

Expectations were high after the Longhorns won the inaugural Big 12 championship in 1996. Texas was ranked No. 11 when the wheels fell off in only the second week of the season as the Horns were demolished 66-3 at home by UCLA. Texas had a meek passing game (quarterback James Brown completed only 49.8 percent of his passes) and the defense, especially the secondary, was awful. The one bright spot was Ricky Williams, who led the NCAA with 1,893 rushing yards in his junior season.

Legendary coaches

University of Texas

Darrell Royal, shown after a victory over Oklahoma in 1958, won three national championships.

Darrell Royal

If there were a Mount Rushmore of UT football coaches in Austin, Royal would get George Washington's primo spot on the left-hand side. Nobody ever meant more to the Texas program than Royal. His mark is all over the team — right down to the helmet logo and the stadium name.

Year	Record	SWC	Rank
1957	6-4-1	4-1-1	11
1958	7-3	3-3	
1959	9-2	5-1	4
1960	7-3-1	5-2	
1961	10-1	6-1	3
1962	9-1-1	6-0-1	4
1963	11-0	7-0	1
1964	10-1	6-1	5
1965	6-4	3-4	
1966	7-4	5-2	
1967	6-4	4-3	
1968	9-1-1	6-1	3
1969	11-0	7-0	1
1970	10-1	7-0	3

ROYALISM

 "I learned this about coaching. You don't have to explain victory and you can't explain defeat."

Mack Brown

Though he led Texas to a BCS championship in the 2005 season, Brown will ultimately be remembered more for the way he rescued and reinvigorated the Texas program. During Brown's tenure, the stadium has undergone massive renovations, the school has established its own TV network and Tex-

Year	Record	SWC	Rank
1998	9-3	6-2	15
1999	9-5	6-2	21
2000	9-3	7-1	12
2001	11-2	7-1	5
2002	11-2	6-2	6
2003	10-3	7-1	12
2004	11-1	7-1	5
2005	13-0	8-0	1
2006	10-3	6-2	13
2007	10-3	5-3	10
2008	12-1	7-1	4
2009	13-1	8-0	2
2010	5-7	2-6	
2011	8-5	4-5	
2012	9-4	5-4	19

as has returned to national prominence. Brown has been a master recruiter and a perfect ambassador for the Longhorns. The only thing he hasn't done consistently is beat Oklahoma.

Fred Akers

The Akers era at Texas was a Dickensian mish-mash of good times and bad times. The coach, an assistant under Darrell Royal and then two seasons as head coach at Wyoming before returning to Austin. He put together national-title contenders in 1978 and 1984, when the Horns went undefeated in the regular season but lost their bowl game both years. That was the rub with

Year	Record	SWC	Rank
1977	11-1	8-0	4
1978	9-3	6-2	9
1979	9-3	6-2	12
1980	7-5	4-4	
1981	10-1-1	6-1-1	2
1982	9-3	7-1	17
1983	11-1	8-0	5
1984	7-4-1	5-3	
1985	8-4	6-2	
1986	5-6	4-4	

Akers — he couldn't win bowl games, going 2-8 and losing four in a row from 1982-85. He also

ROYALISM

"It's like having a big ol' lollipop in your mouth and the first thing you know, all you have is the stick."

on losing the game in the final minutes

struggled against the Barry Switzer-led Sooners and Jackie Sherrill's resurgent Aggies toward the end of his tenure (having gone 1-3-1 in his last five seasons vs. OU and lost the final three A&M games by large margins). The bottom line for Akers: His immediate predecessor, Royal, was too hard an act to follow. Before Akers' final season, the *Houston Chronicle* quoted a UT insider as saying, "Bitching about Fred has become the state's favorite pastime." After 10 years, Akers was fired.

Dana X. Bible

Texas wasn't a nationally recognized team when Bible took over, but by the time he left, the Horns were regularly ranked in the top 15. Bible was elected to the College Football Hall of Fame in 1951.

Year	Record	SWC	Rank
1937	2-6-1	1-5	
1938	1-8	1-5	
1939	5-4	3-3	
1940	8-2	4-2	
1941	8-1-1	4-1-1	4
1942	9-2	5-1	11
1943	7-1-1	5-0	14
1944	5-4	3-2	
1945	10-1	5-1	10
1946	8-2	4-2	5

Clyde Littlefield

Back in the days when coaches did double duty, Littlefield amassed an extraordinary career as a track coach, winning 25 Southwest Conference championships in 41 years. Many people only know his name because

Year	Record	SWC
1927	6-2-1	2-2-1
1928	7-2	5-1
1929	5-2-2	2-2-2
1930	8-1-1	4-1
1931	6-4	2-3
1932	8-2	5-1
1933	4-5-2	2-3-1

of the Texas Relays, which are named after him. But he wasn't half bad as a football coach, either.

All-time NFL team

Offense

QB Bobby Layne (1944-47) The only Longhorns QB ever to be elected to the Pro Football Hall of Fame, Layne played 15 seasons in the NFL. He won three NFL championships as a Detroit Lion and made six Pro Bowls. When he retired, Layne held the NFL career records for passes attempted, passes completed, passing yards and passing touchdowns.

RB Earl Campbell (1974-77) Along with Layne, Campbell is one of two Longhorns elected to the Pro Football Hall of Fame primarily for their contributions as players (Tom Landry and Tex Schramm are in for their roles as the coach and GM of the Dallas Cowboys.) Known for his ferocious, bullish running style, the 232-pound "Tyler

Rose" ran over opponents with abandon in an eight-year NFL career. He won four consecutive AFC rushing titles with the Houston Oilers and finished his career with the New Orleans Saints.

University of Texas

Earl Campbell, who won the Heisman Trophy in 1977, is one of two Longhorns elected to the Pro Football Hall of Fame for his contributions as a player.

RB Ricky Williams (1995-98) The shy, dreadlocked kid from San Diego set the NCAA record for most career yards and won the Heisman Trophy at UT before embarking on a long, sometimes strange trip in the NFL. Williams became the 26th running back to amass 10,000 yards in the NFL, despite not playing at all in 2004 and 2006 and appearing in only one game in 2007 due to violations of the NFL drug policy and a short-lived, self-imposed early retirement.

TE Jermichael Finley (2006-07) After only two years at UT, Finley was ready for the NFL and was selected in the third round by Green Bay. In his first five seasons with the Packers, Finley racked up 198 receptions for 2,485 yards and 17 touchdowns.

OL Jerry Sisemore (1970-72) Sisemore helped UT to three Southwest Conference championships and was a two-time consensus All-American before his productive NFL career began after the Philadelphia Eagles made him the third player selected overall in the 1973 NFL Draft. He lived up to expectations, playing 170 out of 175 games in 12 seasons.

OL Leonard Davis (1997-2000) The 6-foot-6, 375-pound lineman spent 12 years in the NFL, making the Pro Bowl three times. Davis spent four years with the Cowboys and reached the Super Bowl with the San Francisco 49ers in 2013.

OL Dan Neil (1993-96) Neil won back-to-back Super Bowls with the Denver Broncos in 1998 and 1999 and started 104 of 108 games from 1998-2004.

OL Justin Blalock (2003-06) Blalock started 51 consecutive games to end his college career and after the 2012 season, his pro streak stood at 80 — meaning Blalock had started 143 of his past 145 games.

OL Bob McKay (1968-69) Over McKay's two seasons, the Longhorns were 20-1-1 with a national championship and two conference titles. McKay's NFL career was illustrious, too: He played nine seasons with the Cleveland Browns (1970-75) and New England Patriots (1976-78).

WR Roy Williams (2000-03) Over eight NFL seasons, Williams caught 44 TD passes and consistently flashed the "Hook 'em Horns" sign after each score. A seventh-round pick for Detroit, Williams later had three productive seasons with the Cowboys.

WR George Sauer Jr. (1962-64) Sauer was well on his way to becoming one of the NFL's greatest receivers when he retired unexpectedly at age 27. In 84 regular-season games over six seasons (1965-70) with the New York Jets, Sauer caught 309 passes for 4,965 yards and 28 TDs. He was one of Joe Namath's favorite targets.

Defense

DE Brian Orakpo (2005-08) After winning the Nagurski Trophy for the nation's top collegiate defensive player, Orakpo was selected in the first round of the 2009 draft by the Washington Redskins. He made the Pro Bowl in each of his first two seasons, but a pectoral injury wiped out most of his 2012 campaign.

DE Tony Brackens (1993-95) In eight seasons with Jacksonville, Brackens became the Jaguars' all-time leader in sacks (55) and was a Pro Bowler in 1999.

DT Steve McMichael (1975-79) Before he became a professional wrestler, McMichael was the UT team MVP in 1979. Between those jobs, he played 16 NFL seasons, including 13 with the Chicago Bears as a lynchpin of their "46" defense that won Super Bowl XX in 1986.

DT Casey Hampton (1996-2000) Nicknamed "Big Snack," Hampton went to Pittsburgh in the first round in 2001 and played in five Pro Bowls as a Steeler. He recorded the game-sealing sack in Super Bowl XL and won another ring in Super Bowl XLIII.

LB Tommy Nobis (1963-65) The Atlanta Falcons put a lot of faith in Nobis, selecting him with their first-ever draft pick (the NFL's No. 1 pick). Nobis was also picked by the AFL's Oilers, but he chose Atlanta over Houston and immediately made a difference in the expansion Falcons' inaugural season. Nobis was the NFL Rookie of the Year in 1966, reaching the Pro Bowl and racking up 294 combined tackles, still the NFL's single-season record. In 11 years, he led the Falcons in tackles nine times and was named to five Pro Bowls.

LB Derrick Johnson (2001-04) A first-round pick for the Kansas City Chiefs in 2005, Johnson continued to improve as his career evolved. Johnson made the Pro Bowl in 2011 and 2012 and was third in the NFL with 110 solo tackles in 2012.

LB Britt Hager (1986-88) An All-American at Texas, Hager played nine seasons in the NFL with the Eagles, Broncos and Los Angeles Rams.

DB Jerry Gray (1981-84) One of only seven Longhorns to twice earn consensus All-American honors (1983, 1984) and the SWC defensive player of the year both years, Gray played nine years in the NFL and made four Pro Bowls. He was one of 14 members of the 2013 College Football Hall of Fame class.

DB Johnnie Johnson (1976-79) Another College Football Hall of Famer, Johnson played 10 seasons in the NFL, nine with the Los Angeles Rams.

DB Quentin Jammer (1997-01) After being selected by the Chargers fifth overall in the

2002 draft, Jammer moved from safety to cornerback, a position he held for the next 11 seasons in
San Diego. He missed only three starts from 2003-
12, and his 157 games started over that 10-year
period were the most by any NFL cornerback.

DB Raymond Clayborn (1973-76)

Known for his blazing speed (he ran a 9.5-second
100 meters), Clayborn played 13 seasons with the
Patriots (1977-89) and Browns (1990-91). When
he retired, his 36 interceptions were a New England
record.

Special teams

K Phil Dawson (1994-97)

As an undraft-
ed free agent in 1998, Dawson's chances of becoming an NFL mainstay seemed slim. The Oak-
land Raiders signed but eventually waived him.
Dawson kicked for the New England Patriots'
practice squad but didn't make the team. In 1999,
the Cleveland Browns signed Dawson and he re-
warded them by becoming the franchise's all-time

leader in field goals made, booting 305 in 14 seasons with the Browns.

P Russell Erxleben (1976-78) The Saints drafted him in the first round — a rarity for a special teams player — and though Erxleben never measured up to that level, he was a decent punter from 1980-83 for New Orleans.

KR/PR Eric Metcalf (1985-88) A four-time track All-American, Metcalf was an incredibly versatile athlete. He was the NCAA champion long jumper twice before he became a first-round draft pick for the Browns. He ran 12 punt/kickoff returns back for touchdowns (the third most in NFL history) and retired in the top 10 all-time in career all-purpose yards (17,230).

HONOR ROLL
National award winners

Heisman Trophy (Best College Player): Earl Campbell (1977), Ricky Williams (1998)

Maxwell Award (Best College Player): Tommy Nobis (1965), Ricky Williams (1998), Vince Young (2005), Colt McCoy, (2009)

Walter Camp Award (Best College Player): Ricky Williams, (1998), Colt McCoy (2008), Colt McCoy (2009)

Davey O'Brien Award (Best Quarterback): Vince Young (2005), Colt McCoy (2009)

Doak Walker Award (Best Running Back): Ricky Williams (1997), Ricky Williams (1998), Cedric Benson, 2004

Jim Thorpe Award (Best Defensive Back): Michael Huff (2005), Aaron Ross, (2006).

Outland Trophy (Best Lineman): Scott Appleton (1963), Tommy Nobis (1965), Brad Shearer (1977)

Vince Lombardi Award (Best Lineman): Kenneth Sims (1981), Tony Degrate (1984), Brian Orakpo (2008)

Bronko Nagurski Award (Best Defensive Player): Derrick Johnson (2004), Brian Orakpo (2008)

Dick Butkus Award (Best Linebacker): Derrick Johnson (2004)

Ted Hendricks Award (Best Defensive End): Brian Orakpo (2008)

Campbell Trophy (Best Scholar-Athlete — "The Academic Heisman"): Sam Acho (2010)

Frank Broyles Award (Best Assistant Coach): Greg Davis (2005)

Index

About the author

Dave Sessions was a freshman at the University of Texas when James Brown rolled left to lead the Longhorns to the 1996 Big 12 championship,

Gary Brown

and he distinctly remembers being part of a small crowd of students who attempted to tear down the goalposts at Memorial Stadium after the game (which was in St. Louis!).

Sessions went on to cover Longhorns sports for *The Daily Texan*, later holding the managing editor position there, before graduating with a journalism degree in 2001. He worked as a sports journalist for the *Austin American-Statesman* and the *Fort Worth Star-Telegram*, where he covered the Dallas Stars and Texas Rangers beats.

After leaving newspapers, Sessions was a staffer for presidential campaigns in 2008 and 2012, then went to Capitol Hill between elections as a congressional press secretary. Based in Fort Worth, he is now a marketing director for a medical devices manufacturer and freelance writer.